HERE TODAY
————————AND——————————
GONE TODAY

The Life of a Widow

Teresa Everett Horne

Paperback ISBN: 979-8-9889181-5-8

To request permissions, contact the author at email: divinepurpose08@yahoo.com

Published & Printed by:

BWE Publishing & Consulting

Raleigh, NC

Table of Contents

Special Thanks...5

Introduction Here Today and Gone Today The Life of a Widow...9

Chapter One Love at First Sight 12

Chapter Two There's Going to Be a Wedding 17

Chapter Three It's Church Decoration and Rehearsal Time.19

Chapter Four The Big Day: Here Comes the Bride 21

Chapter Five The Honeymoon...............................25

Chapter Six The Journey Begins for Mr. and Mrs. Gregory Thomas Horne Sr. 28

Chapter Seven The Blessings of the Married Life 30

Chapter Eight Marriage and Ministry of God's Servants 34

Chapter Nine Gregory and His Community Involvement 41

Chapter Ten Gregory, the Detention Officer 45

Chapter Eleven Passion for His Career................................48

Chapter Twelve Career Achievements and Promotion.........52

Chapter Thirteen That One Day That Shifted His Career.....56

Chapter Fourteen "The Leading Up" Days............................59

Chapter Fifteen The Day and the Days That Changed My Entire Life..63

Chapter Sixteen Lord, Why?..70

Chapter Seventeen Lord, Where Do I Go From Here?.........74

Chapter Eighteen The Widow Life..78

Chapter Nineteen Not My Will But Thy Will Be Done 86

♪ There's a Story Behind My Praise 89

♪ I Feel Like Going On 90

Special Facebook Tributes...92

Children's Tribute..96

My Special Family Tribute 101

In Loving Memory..103

The Life of Gregory Thomas Horne Sr...............................104

About the Author 110

Special Thanks

Special thanks to all our family, friends, loved ones, law enforcement agencies, and the many organizations around the world who support officers who have fallen in the line of duty. Thank you all for embracing and loving us during such a sudden, unexpected, and difficult time and even now, as we navigate this new chapter of our lives.

I thank God for my children, Gregory Jr. and Alexus, who stood with me and continue to stand with me. They are constantly checking on me and making sure I'm all right, and I do the same for them. We share memories, laugh, cry, and often say we wish it didn't have to be this way. But we don't falsely accuse God. Instead, we're learning day by day to say, "God knows what He's doing," the title of my husband's last message that he preached.

I thank God for Sheriff Cleveland "Clee" Atkinson and the entire staff of the Edgecombe County Sheriff's Office. These impressive men and women have stood with my family and me from the very beginning. They stay in constant contact, regularly checking on the children just as a loving family would. They kept me informed about events that honored my husband and ensured I could attend those held outside our local area and in other states. They've stood by us, and we are deeply appreciative.

Detention Corporal Officer Gregory T. Horne (J54) loved his Sheriff, his job, and his co-workers. Not a day went by that he didn't pray for them. In fact, I would often hear him praying two or three times a day, sometimes more. I can still see him now, sitting in the car with his head bowed and his hands lifted in prayer before driving off. When he came home from his shift, he would pray again for those still working. At night, before bed, he'd pray once more. He truly covered you all in much prayer!

Mr. Gene Harrell, former Chief Deputy at the Sheriff's Office—thank you so much for your quick response to our home when Alexus and I needed someone to comfort and console us. Even now, I can hear your voice saying how sorry you were. I can still see the sadness on your face, hear the crack in your voice, and recall the redness in your eyes. Thank you for staying with my daughter and me until others arrived. I'm truly grateful.

Curmilus "Butch" Dancy II, just having to ask Alexus to call you and tell you what was happening was incredibly painful. Even now, I can feel the disbelief and hurt in your heart. All I know is that you showed up quickly, fast, and in a hurry. I can still see the sorrow on your face and the disbelief in your eyes. You and Greg were cousins, but more like brothers. He thought so highly of you. Whether you know it or not, I would often hear him praying for you during his prayer time. He respected you deeply.

Thank you for being there for us then and for continuing to be there for the children and me.

Thank you for being present at the homegoing service and the repast, doing what you do best capturing moments through photos and video. Thank you for the delicious grilled food and for your support at events honoring him. Thank you for looking out for me and checking on the children.

To President Dr. Greg McLeod and the Edgecombe Community College, Tarboro Campus thank you so much for blessing our family with access to the Keihin Auditorium. My husband loved the community college and was always willing to help in whatever capacity he could. He would recruit students by sharing his experiences at the college. I used to joke with him and say he should apply for a position there. He'd just smile and say, "I got this!" So again, thank you all so much for everything.

To our wonderful neighbors, Mr. Clifton and Mrs. Shelley Lashley, thank you both for everything you've done and continue to do for me. Every act of kindness has been, and still is, so deeply appreciated. Having good neighbors is more important than ever in times like these, and I'm truly grateful to God for you both. I know my husband would be happy knowing you've helped me in so many ways.

To all the pastors, churches, organizations, towns, cities, and communities both near and far who prayed for and supported us: thank you all so very much.

Last, but certainly not least, my family and I thank God for giving us His much-needed love, grace, mercy, strength, peace, and comfort during such an unexpected and heartbreaking time. We could not have made it without God carrying us through. Even now, He remains the source of our strength, and we give Him all the glory, honor, and praise even in this and after this. We thank You, Lord Jesus!

Introduction
Here Today and Gone Today
The Life of a Widow

The precious gift of life is something we should all cherish and be thankful for. Every day, we should learn to love more, make lasting memories, and never take for granted the people in our lives because we never know when our time on this earth will come to an end.

There's a common saying: *"Here today and gone tomorrow."* But I've come to understand it as *"Here Today And Gone Today."*

As James 4:14 (KJV) says:

"Whereas ye know not what shall be on the morrow. For what is your life? It is even a vapour, that appeareth for a little time, and then vanisheth away."

In other words, we must hold on to what truly matters, because time is slipping away every second, every minute, every hour of the day and night. Some may not view life this way, but the truth is: our lives are entirely in God's hands. He is the one who gives us our days, and He is the one who can take them away. So, can you see just how life really is a gift from God?

In this book, I will share the journey that my family and I have had to endure only by the grace of God. This journey includes the sudden and unexpected transition of my husband and their dad, Gregory Thomas Horne Sr., on September 25, 2022. I will also speak about the transitions of some of my other dearest loved ones.

Additionally, I'll share godly wisdom about death and grief, and what the Word of God says about how we, as believers in Jesus Christ, are to cope with these painful realities.

I will be as transparent as I can so that my life story might become a testimony that helps bring healing and deliverance to others who may face or are already facing similar trials. I'll share some of my most difficult daily struggles and how the Holy Spirit helps me overcome the negative thoughts, emotions, and feelings that try to take hold. I'll also offer personal life lessons I've passed on to others, in hopes of helping them better prepare for the moments when death comes into their lives.

As I kept saying "in this book," I hadn't yet mentioned the title because the Lord had not revealed it to me. But as I was writing, the Holy Spirit suddenly gave it to me. I shared it with my daughter, and she replied: *"I LIKE THAT!"* And so, the rest is history.

Here Today and Gone Today The Life of a Widow

I pray and believe that this book will bless many people and bring renewed hope, encouragement, wisdom, and knowledge to those who are experiencing death and grief.

I also pray that many will come to receive the gift of salvation from the one who gave us this precious gift of life and who alone has the authority to take it away.

I pray and believe that many will be strengthened and comforted, knowing that God is our refuge and strength, a very present help in trouble (Psalm 46:1, KJV).

So, as you prepare to read this book, I want you to know: no matter what you're going through right now whether it's death and grief or something else God loves you, He cares about you, and He is going to carry you through whatever you're facing.

Also, I want you to know that I love you in the Lord Jesus Christ. And finally, know this: I am praying for you and your family. Continue to be encouraged and strengthened in the Lord Jesus Christ, for in Him we live, and move, and have our being (Acts 17:28, KJV).

Chapter One
Love at First Sight

It was in April of 2011 when I began receiving private messages on Facebook from a young man named Gregory Thomas Horne. Not only was I getting messages, but he was consistently following my page. His name kept popping up through his *comments, shares,* and *likes.* I started to get a little curious about who he was and what he wanted—as if I didn't already know (lol).

One day, I finally gave in and started talking with him via Facebook Messenger. We continued our conversations and eventually exchanged phone numbers. It wasn't long before my phone rang—and it was him. We talked for an hour that first day, and before hanging up, he asked when he could call again. *Lord, have mercy!* This young man was more serious about me than I thought.

After weeks of talking on the phone and sharing our lives with one another, he learned that I needed some things for my home. When I shared this with him, he told me that he was in the process of moving, and what I needed—he was willing to share with me. *Lord, have mercy,* things were moving so fast. I agreed, and he asked when he could bring the items over. We set a time, and sure enough, he and a friend arrived at my house to unload everything—right on schedule.

In my mind, I was saying, *"This guy is serious."*

That Saturday morning, as they arrived, my daughter Alexus and I were sitting at the computer. She looked out and asked, *"Who is that man?"* At the time, she didn't know I'd been talking to him, and she was only thirteen years old. Naturally, she was curious. As a single mom, I hadn't brought any men around her—much less into our home. I explained a little to her while they were unloading, and she seemed content with our conversation.

When they finished placing the items where they belonged, Gregory came into the den where Alexus and I were. He introduced himself and we talked briefly. Since he was with a friend, he didn't want to keep him waiting, so we agreed to meet again soon when we'd have more time.

Our next planned meeting was just a few days later—on his lunch break. We had already made the arrangements ahead of time. That day, we met at Indian Lake Park, had lunch, and continued getting to know each other.

Our primary conversation was about our faith. He learned that I was a preacher in the Lord's Church, and I learned that he was a Christian and a *Deacon in Training* at his church. That was important to both of us, because an unequally yoked relationship would never have worked—God would not have allowed it. We talked about many things, and as his lunch break ended, he asked when we could see each other again. We planned our next "date."

Lord, have mercy, things were still moving fast—but one thing gave me confidence: as I prayed and sought God about Gregory and me, the Lord kept giving me peace and confirmation. So, I trusted God and continued forward.

It turned out to be a wonderful time for both of us. Gregory was mannerable, polite, and humble in spirit. He also built a relationship with my daughter, which made her feel good about us being friends. As she "assessed" him, she quickly had him wrapped around her finger. Sometimes he'd ask her if she wanted anything, and she'd put him to the test and say, *"Yes."* He'd ask what she wanted, and she'd tell him.

Lo and behold, he'd bring her exactly what she loved— McDonald's chicken nuggets and French fries. In her thirteen-year-old mind, that made him a *"nice man."* And it didn't happen just once. Anytime she wanted something, he got it for her. He did the same for me. *Lord, have mercy,* things are still moving fast!

After about four months of spending time together and growing closer, Gregory became even more serious. In August, he popped the question. I was shocked—but I also knew it was God's doing. I had been constantly in prayer about the relationship, having been single for so long. I needed to be sure that Gregory was *God-sent*, and not just another "fly-by-night guy."

Through my praying and fasting, the Lord continued to confirm that he was the one. I asked Gregory to give me some time to process everything and to talk it over with Alexus, since she was the one living with me at the time. He agreed.

I spent time sharing with Alexus, answering her questions as best I could. She was excited and happy for us. Then Gregory and I sat down with her together to hear her final thoughts. We were all excited, and so—I accepted his proposal.

From meeting and having lunch in April of 2011, to getting engaged in August of that same year, ours was a fast-moving relationship. But we truly saw and felt the hand of God in it.

At first, we didn't tell many people—and most of you can probably understand why. We wanted to be sure we were moving in God's timing, so that everything would unfold as He intended.

After much prayer and seeking the Lord, we chose our wedding date: November 5, 2011. We were so excited about what the Lord had done—and what He was continuing to do.

Chapter Two
There's Going to Be a Wedding

In the weeks and months leading up to the wedding, Gregory purchased my engagement ring, and we began sharing the news with our family, friends, and loved ones. We had our engagement printed in the local newspaper, obtained our marriage license, and dove into wedding planning.

Oh and by the way my mom was the seamstress for all the women's dresses!

To our amazement, almost everyone was happy for us. We knew some might not be, but that didn't discourage or deter us. We continued to seek the Lord's guidance every step of the way, and He truly blessed us.

During the planning phase, every single person we invited to participate in the wedding graciously said "yes." Gregory and I began to discuss our desired wedding colors, and the Lord revealed them to us. We prayed about the venue and reached out to the pastor of the church and she graciously gave us permission to have the wedding there.

We prayed about who should serve as our Wedding Director, and when we reached out to her, she was ecstatic and said "yes!" Everyone we asked to be part of the wedding whether in the wedding party, or helping behind the scenes responded with such enthusiasm and joy.

The officiant, the seamstress, the videographer and photographer, the musician and singer, the reception emcee and servers, the ushers, and even the cleanup crew all said yes.

Everything was falling beautifully into place, and we knew the hand of God was on our soon-to-be marriage.

The months flew by quickly, and soon it was time to bring everything together. We met with the wedding party to discuss their roles and attire, and they wasted no time doing what was needed. Gregory and I had already purchased our wedding outfits and accessories, secured the rental equipment, and gathered the decorations for the church.

We also purchased our rings, met with the reception crew to finalize the menu, and before we knew it we were ready for the wedding rehearsal.

Chapter Three
It's Church Decoration and Rehearsal Time

At this point, we had gathered all the church decorations, and the Lord blessed us to put everything together in such a beautiful way. We had the best Wedding Director, along with the full support of our wedding party and the results were truly impressive.

The church was already beautifully set up with decor that matched our colors, which made the process even smoother. God was clearly orchestrating this wedding from beginning to end.

After the decorating was complete, we prepared for the rehearsal. Everyone there was excited and a little nervous at the same time. Gregory opened with a prayer, and then we turned things over to our Director.

She started by having everyone introduce themselves, since not everyone knew each other. That moment brought a sense of ease and connection. We even had some laughs as she paired the bridesmaids and groomsmen especially because we had people of such *varied* heights! It made the pairing process all the more fun.

Once everyone was lined up properly, our Director began the walk-through. It only took three practice runs and boom we had it down pat. Even the little participants did an amazing job!

Things were continuing to move so quickly, and the hand of God was clearly upon this wedding. Everyone was amazed by how smoothly things went and how well everyone worked together with a spirit of excellence.

Once the rehearsal concluded, I offered the closing prayer. We were dismissed with hearts full of excitement and anticipation for the big day ahead.

Chapter Four
The Big Day: Here Comes the Bride

Oh my goodness things were happening so fast! Where did the time go? It seemed like it was still April when we first met, but now it was November 5th, 2011, and it was our BIG DAY!!!

The wedding was scheduled for 2:00 p.m. The guys were off doing their "thing," and so were the ladies. My cousin Reneika did my hair early that morning, and I was absolutely *so* excited. The wedding party arrived at the church at noon to begin getting dressed. Praise God, everyone made it!

All of the ladies were so instrumental in helping me get ready—hair, dress, makeup everything was top-notch. The clock was ticking, and we were all just bubbling over with excitement.

Gregory and I hadn't expected a large wedding. We didn't send out formal invitations because we knew the church was big enough, and our amazing reception crew had everything under control in terms of food and setup.

As it got closer to 2:00pm, our Wedding Director began preparing everyone for the ceremony lineup. By then, I was honestly getting nervous. In the back, just before walking down the aisle, I took one last glance in the mirror and I must say I was an incredibly beautiful bride.

Now it was 2:00pm. The procession was about to begin. I heard the music start, and all I could do was smile. The ceremony had officially begun and was moving right along. Before I knew it, it was time for the bride to make her grand entrance.

With my son, Dee, on my right arm and my uncle Ronnie on my left, I was nervous but so incredibly happy. When the doors opened and I looked inside the church, I locked eyes with Gregory and then saw the sea of people gathered. My heart was overflowing with joy. The church was packed on both sides.

I pulled myself together, lifted my head high, and strutted confidently down that aisle. *It was on and poppin' now!*

The ceremony went so smoothly, everything went just as planned. We had the best Wedding Director, Sharon Jones, and the most supportive wedding party anyone could ask for. Then it was time for photos and all the fun before the reception festivities.

After we had our fill of photos and laughter, we prepared for the reception lineup and it was *so much fun*. The entire wedding party, including the beautiful bride and handsome groom, made our own personalized swag entrances, which drew cheers and laughter from the guests.

Once everyone was in, the reception crew blessed the food and gave instructions for serving. The food was plentiful and beautifully presented. The aroma was mouthwatering, and it tasted every bit as delicious as it looked.

As we ate, there was singing and dancing. Gregory and I toasted and shared our cake-cutting moment. Everyone had a blast, and the love in the room throughout the entire day was simply amazing.

Gregory and I were deeply appreciative of everything that had transpired—from the day of our engagement announcement to that very moment. God had been so faithful to us.

This wedding was truly ordained by God—and He did it quickly!

Then came honeymoon time!

As usual, everything had been very well planned in such a short period. The Lord favored us so much that our entire wedding cost only $1,300.00. Our reception crew even blessed us by covering the full cost of the menu.

The favor of God was all over our wedding and marriage.

As Proverbs 18:22 (KJV) declares:

"He who finds a wife finds a good thing, and obtains favor from the Lord."

To God be all the glory!

Chapter Five
The Honeymoon

The Lord had brought us through such a beautiful wedding, surrounded by so many of our family members and friends—and now it was time for the newlyweds to embark on that special journey called the honeymoon, a time to celebrate our love, unity, and quality time together.

We were so excited, especially after witnessing all that the Lord had done for us in such a short time. We chose Virginia Beach, Virginia as our honeymoon destination and left for our trip a couple of weeks after the wedding celebration.

We arrived safely, unpacked, and began the journey of relaxing, spending time together, and adjusting to our new life as husband and wife. It was a season of discovery—getting to know one another more deeply and learning what it meant to walk together in marriage.

Once again, Gregory and I talked about our faith in God. First and foremost, we had both agreed that our faith would be the foundation of a strong and lasting marriage. We knew that God had to be at the center of everything.

We held tight to Ecclesiastes 4:12 (NLT):

> *"A person standing alone can be attacked and defeated, but two can stand back-to-back and conquer. Three are even better, for a triple-braided cord is not easily broken."*

We knew that God was that triple-braided cord, and with Him, our marriage would be secured and upheld.

We talked about our children and families, and the roles they would play in our marriage. We reflected on how we met, and we shared our hopes and dreams for the future. We truly opened our hearts to each other and embraced this new chapter called "marriage."

We spent quality time walking the beach, eating at various restaurants, shopping, watching TV, and simply enjoying the comfort of each other's presence. It was the holiday season, so the area was beautifully decorated with Christmas lights—even though it was Thanksgiving.

My birthday was on the 28th, so we celebrated both my birthday and our first Thanksgiving together. The beach and boardwalk were especially magical at night, and we enjoyed evening strolls along the shore and through the downtown mall. We had so much fun together—it felt like we'd known each other for years.

Through our conversations, Gregory learned that I loved crab legs—and, being the gentleman he was, he found a Captain George's restaurant and took me there. We had a blast! The staff learned we were newlyweds and surprised us with a birthday song and dance. It was a moment I'll never forget.

As our honeymoon days began to wind down, we knew it was time to prepare for our return home—to step fully into our new life as husband and wife. We had thoroughly enjoyed our time away and prayed that God would continue to bless our union.

Finally, the day came to leave our honeymoon getaway. Of course, we thanked God for blessing us with such meaningful time together. We had made precious memories, and now we were heading back home.

God granted us traveling grace and mercy, and we returned safely with everything intact.

Praise God from whom all blessings flow!
It was a wonderful time of bonding as husband and wife!

Chapter Six
The Journey Begins for Mr. and Mrs. Gregory Thomas Horne Sr.

According to *Merriam-Webster*, a journey is defined as something that suggests travel or passage from one place to another—an act or instance of moving from one place to another. Marriage truly is a journey, because it's not something that happens overnight.

Although we had spent a few wonderful weeks together on our honeymoon, there was still so much we had to learn and adjust to. This was just the beginning of our journey—and we were excited.

Marriage is about taking things one day at a time, learning how to adjust to a new lifestyle, and discovering ways of doing things that work best for everyone involved. Gregory and I knew that we both needed to be patient and understanding with one another, so we continually sought the Lord through prayer as we built our marriage.

Because Alexus was part of our household at the time, we made sure to involve her in some of the things we did as a couple. Everything we did—we prayed about it—and the Holy Spirit led and guided us.

Gregory and Alexus connected really well, and yes, he spoiled her too. We had so much fun together as a family—going on trips, dining at restaurants, visiting Greg Jr. in Maryland, and taking part in all kinds of adventurous outings.

Alexus would occasionally "test" Gregory, just to *check him out*—and each time, he came through for her. Over time, their bond grew stronger, and we truly blessed God for that. We wanted our household to be unified and in harmony under God.

As we continued to build our life together, we found ourselves making many adjustments—normal, typical things that most newlyweds experience as they settle into their shared life.

The Lord continued to bless us with everything we needed in this early stage of our marriage.

Chapter Seven
The Blessings of the Married Life

As the days, weeks, and months went by, our marriage began to fall into place—as if we had been together for years. We found ourselves living, loving, and laughing for real. We lived life to the fullest, laughing and sharing God's love with each other and with everyone we encountered.

Every move we made, we sought the Lord. Every decision we faced, we sought the Lord.

We didn't just laugh during the good times—we also learned to laugh through the challenges. We made a conscious effort to spread God's love wherever we went. We always tried to look for the good and the positive in everything and everyone.

When we made mistakes, we learned from them, let go of the past, and moved forward. We learned to truly listen to one another and, in turn, to do what was best for our family. We encouraged each other and lifted one another up—even when unexpected situations and trials came our way. We lived a life of hope and faith in God.

Gregory was such a humble and respectful young man. Even before we were married, he demonstrated the very character of God. He was a true family man, and I loved that about him. He always put his family before himself. He was a great provider and protector—making sure we were well taken care of.

He made it easy to love him and easy to live with him, just as God intended marriage to be. Watching how he cared for our family inspired me to step up my game and treat him with an even greater level of love, respect, and appreciation.

Gregory had a genuine heart for people, even when he wasn't genuinely loved, respected, or appreciated in return. He was never swayed by others' opinions or judgments. He would always say: "To God be all the glory!"

As a stay-at-home wife and mom, I was blessed to care for my family every single day—and I did it as unto the Lord. I made sure they had everything they needed, and I did it with a spirit of excellence. The Lord truly gave me the strength and grace to do it all.

The best part of being at home was seeing them off each day for work and school—and being there to greet them when they returned. I was able to prepare breakfast, lunch, and dinner for them daily. I loved being able to provide this kind of ministry of care for my family.

Gregory would often say: "To God be all the glory!"

When he was off work, we spent lots of quality time together as a family. We took trips to Maryland to visit Greg Jr., and sometimes he would come down to spend time with us. We loved those moments together.

We also traveled to Wrightsville Beach near Wilmington, North Carolina; Oceanfront Beach in Virginia Beach, Virginia; and Myrtle Beach, South Carolina, where we visited the Hollywood Wax Museum. We even attended an NFL game in Charlotte, North Carolina—and we had a blast!

Gregory made our lives enjoyable and fun, and just like always, he'd say: "To God be all the glory!"

He enjoyed grilling, and we'd often find ourselves in friendly grill competitions—because he was convinced he was better than me. *Oh really?* (LOL) Yes, he truly believed it! I let him prove it, and in the process, I boosted his confidence so much that he wanted to grill all the time. Eventually, I gave in and told him, "You win—you're better!" And of course, he responded, "To God be all the glory!"

Gregory loved chicken, especially fried chicken—and he could've eaten it every single day! I made sure to cook his favorite at least once or twice a week. He truly deserved it.

We had a great married life. Not once did Gregory raise his voice or argue. He always said what he needed to say and then gave it to the Lord.

He was just a great man.

Chapter Eight
Marriage and Ministry of God's Servants

At the beginning of our marriage, Gregory and I were attending separate places of worship. We both believed that God would have us worship together, but we weren't sure how that was to come about. So, we sought the Lord through prayer and fasting.

After hearing from the Lord, it became clear that I was to join Gregory at the church where he was attending. We did what we needed to do to make the transition as smooth as possible. Of course, it was difficult for me, but I had to obey the Lord's instructions.

At the time of the transition, I was an ordained Evangelist in the Lord's church, and Gregory was a Deacon in Training at his local assembly. As I connected with the ministry, it quickly became evident why the Lord had me there with him: we began to grow and mature in the Lord together as a couple.

While Gregory was training to become a Deacon, the Lord allowed me to support him in his studies. When he had to teach Bible study or minister the Word, I often supported his assignments by ministering in song. God used me to help set the atmosphere for the Word to go forth—wherein miracles of healing and deliverance would take place.

Gregory was eventually ordained as a Deacon in the Lord's church, and God used him mightily in that role. There was so much growth and development in that ministry for both of us.

Not long after connecting there, the Lord opened the door for me to minister the Word, and I was both grateful and humbled. Gregory and I began to minister as a team, and the Lord blessed us and the people during our time there. We recognized and accepted that marriage is a ministry in itself, and we continued to seek the Lord for guidance and instruction.

As we continued growing in ministry together, the Lord transitioned us to another level—this time, by moving us to a new ministry. What we didn't fully realize at the time was that God was ordering our steps for our specific callings and Kingdom assignments.

Once again, we submitted to our new leadership and followed the Lord's instructions. We were faithful and dedicated—not looking for positions or titles, but simply wanting to walk in obedience to God.

Little did we know, the steps we were taking were being divinely orchestrated by the Lord. As we sat under our then-leaders, the Lord was still grooming and preparing us for our destiny.

It wasn't long before God opened more doors. We began ministering the Word on several occasions, were assigned to the Evangelistic Outreach Ministry, and I served in the Intercessory Prayer Ministry. Again, the Lord was shaping us for our calling.

We remained in that ministry until the Lord directed us to another place of growth and development—one where He would begin positioning us as the leaders He was calling us to be.

We obeyed the Lord's instructions and entered our next place of spiritual growth. Once again, we were faithful and dedicated not only to the Lord, but to the leaders who covered our family and ministry. We sat, listened, and grew through the teaching and training provided.

As before, we weren't looking for elevation, just to do the will of God. But soon after arriving, we were given ministry assignments, and the Lord blessed us to fulfill them with a spirit of excellence.

A few years later on August 14, 2016 our then-spiritual covering leaders ordained us both into the Pastoral office of ministry. This was a major milestone in our lives. We knew God had a plan concerning our call to ministry, and now He was manifesting it.

By this point, I had been ordained as an Evangelist, and Gregory had been ordained as a Deacon. But the Lord had to take us through a specific path of preparation to bring us into Pastoral leadership.

We continued to sit under those leaders and grew even more. For four years, we served however we were asked—until the Lord transitioned us again, this time to a higher level of spiritual development.

We then came under a new set of spiritual covering leaders and remained faithful there as well. We attended various training and equipping sessions as time permitted. We matured in the Apostolic and Prophetic offices through the School of the Apostles and Prophets. It was a powerful season of preparation, and we were blessed to receive such vital teaching.

The instruction and training helped us walk confidently in the Kingdom mandate God had ordained for our lives.

On August 23, 2020, Gregory and I were once again ordained in the Lord's church. He was ordained as an Apostolic Pastor, and I was affirmed and ordained into the Office of the Prophet. What a blessing from the Lord that was!

In August 2022, we made our final spiritual covering transition—again, led by the Lord. We remained faithful and supportive, using all of the teaching and training we had received over the years under amazing spiritual leaders. Each one played a significant part in preparing us for our God-ordained calling.

Some may say we moved between ministries and spiritual coverings often—and yes, we did. But we did so under the leading of the Holy Spirit.

I often compare our transitions in the ministry to that of the school system: you don't stay in the same grade or with the same teacher for twelve years. You progress. As you grow and pass each level, you move on—and that's exactly what we did in ministry.

Some have asked why spiritual coverings are important especially when we were already leaders of our own ministry. The answer is accountability. In ministry, there must be oversight. We always had spiritual leaders who held us accountable not just to them, but to God. They taught us to walk in character and integrity, and we gave them no reason to doubt us. We honored and respected them fully.

The Lord blessed us with our own ministry space in June 2022, and we were so excited about what God had done. We had been faithful and patient in our season of waiting, and now God's perfect timing had arrived.

He gave us favor with man, and we were able to set up the building in a spirit of excellence. We began hosting services-our very own moves of God and the people in attendance were truly blessed. God was glorified.

We also began to carry out the work of the Evangelist in our commUNITY, reaching souls for the Kingdom and drawing them into the House of the Lord for discipleship and equipping.

The Lord was ordering our steps and we obeyed Him. Souls were being saved and transformed. Most of all, God was glorified. We were truly blessed by everything God was doing in that season of our lives.

Side   note: During all our years under spiritual leadership, we were already hosting moves of God in our home, and renting spaces for commUNITY events as the Lord led. That's how He instructed us to begin our ministry.

We held Bible studies, completed outreach assignments, and stayed faithful to the structure God had given us. We hosted events like:

- Back-to-School giveaways

- Coats for Kids

- Food, clothing, and personal toiletries distributions

- Thanksgiving and Christmas giveaways

- Emergency financial assistance, as the Lord directed

We were trusted by God because our hearts were pure and sincere toward His people.

And so, He blessed us—not only to have our own ministry, but also to remain faithful and supportive to every spiritual covering we were under.

We truly made an impact for the Kingdom of God—and all the glory belongs to Him!

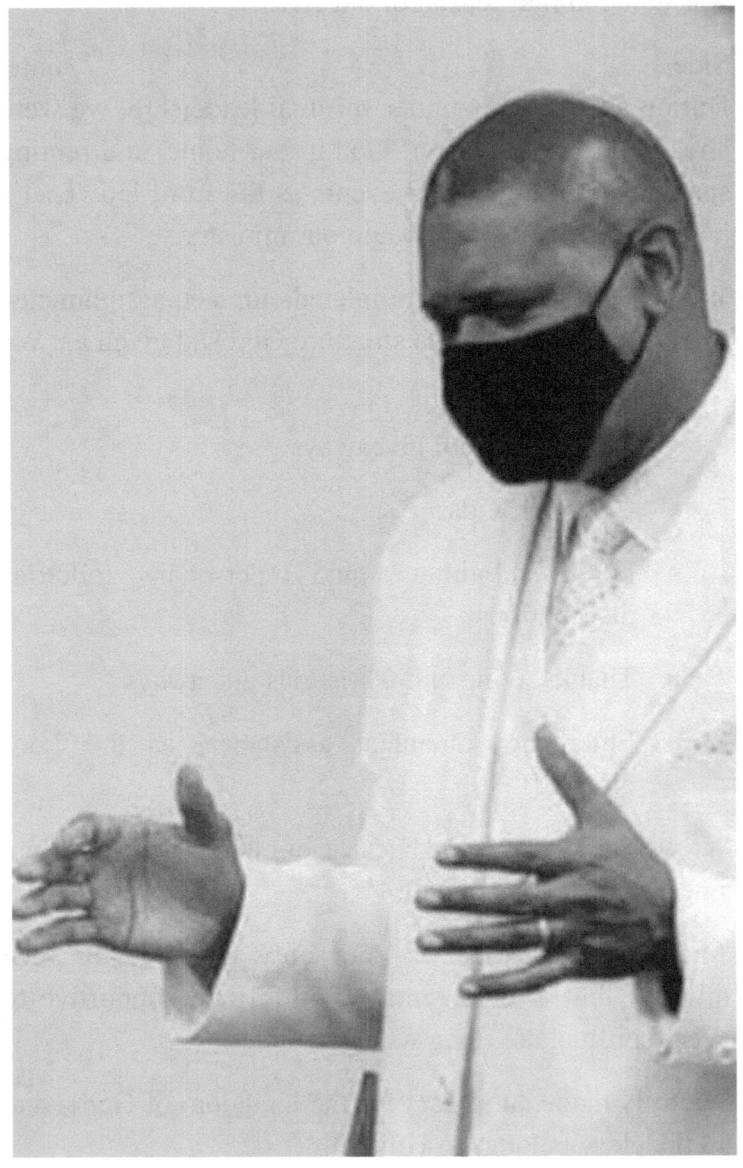

Chapter Nine
Gregory and His Community Involvement

Gregory was a highly active citizen in the community. His love for God and people inspired him to get involved in various events, organizations, and service projects.

While attending Edgecombe Community College, he served as Chapter President of the Alpha Omega Nu Chapter of Phi Theta Kappa International Honor Society. According to the Edgecombe Community College website, Phi Theta Kappa is an international honor society that *"recognizes and encourages the academic achievement of two-year college students and provides opportunities for individual growth and development through honors, leadership, and service programming."*

During his tenure, Gregory assisted with several community service initiatives, including:

- Relay for Life

- Adopt-A-Highway cleanups

- Textbook recycling drives

41

- Food drive distribution to families in the local community

In partnership with our outreach ministry, EndTime Harvest Outreach Ministries, Gregory also collaborated with the chapter to provide back-to-school supplies for foster care children through the Edgecombe County Department of Human Services. That particular project was one he especially enjoyed.

When approached by the chapter's advisor, Mrs. Tamara Frank-Pourvady, to serve as Chapter President, Gregory was initially unsure if he was capable of fulfilling the role. But after much encouragement from her, he accepted and as we can see from all he accomplished, he did an amazing job. Mrs. Frank-Pourvady was so proud of him.

Gregory had already formed a close friendship with Dr. Gregory McLeod, President of Edgecombe Community College. However, this leadership role brought them even closer.

He was also involved with the Edgecombe Community College Foundation Annual Golf Tournament. Gregory happily assisted wherever and however they needed him. He especially enjoyed this project because he had recently purchased golf clubs and was beginning to practice and develop his skills during his personal time.

In addition to his educational and outreach efforts, Gregory participated in community events connected to his career in law enforcement. He attended and assisted with National Night Out events, which are typically held in August each year.

These events are designed to build stronger relationships between community members and law enforcement agencies—including local police departments and sheriff's offices. The focus is on encouraging community involvement in preventing crime and promoting safety.

At one of the events, Gregory volunteered to help with face painting, and he enjoyed it so much, it seemed like the beginning of a fun new hobby! He always looked forward to these gatherings because they gave him the chance to meet people and build connections. Gregory was truly a "people person" through and through.

Gregory was also active in local politics through the Edgecombe County Democratic Party. He was passionate about educating and inspiring citizens to take active roles in the political process. He especially loved seeing both young people and seniors getting involved.

He attended Democratic Party meetings both virtually and in person. During his time with the Edgecombe County Democratic Party, Gregory served as:

- Precinct 1-4 Chair

- Treasurer/Secretary of the County Executive Committee for six years

His service was deeply appreciated. Gregory was highly organized and methodical—traits that made him an excellent fit for these roles. He even kept meticulous records at home, and that same level of excellence and attention to detail showed in his service with the party.

Chapter Ten
Gregory, the Detention Officer

At the beginning of our marriage, Gregory was employed with CopyPro, Inc., a Greenville, North Carolina–based company that provided office automation technology services including printing, copying, and scanning. He worked as an IT Copier Technician, and he absolutely loved his job, his co-workers, and the customers he served.

I never once heard him speak negatively or complain about his job. Once again, he showed me his true character. He was just an unusual kind of guy—in the best way—and I blessed the Lord for him.

A few years into our marriage, Gregory and I were watching television and enjoying some family time when, out of the blue, I told him that I could see him working in some form of law enforcement. I had no idea where the thought came from or why I said it—but I said it.

His response was, of course: "To God be all the glory!"

I looked at him and started to laugh, because I had been expecting a different kind of response. I told him I was serious. He asked why I would say something like that—

and at the time, I truly didn't know. I knew he was content with his current job, so it made no logical sense.

But later, I came to understand: it was God leading me to speak that into his life.

We discussed it and prayed about it and in God's perfect timing, it manifested.

In 2015, Gregory joined the Edgecombe County Sheriff's Office as a Detention Officer.

Gregory was so excited about this "new job," as we called it at first. Although he wasn't entirely sure about the move he had just made, he quickly realized that it was God who had granted him favor and opened this new door. Eventually, he stopped calling it a "job" and started calling it his career.

There was a training process he had to go through, which included both a physical training component and a written test. Gregory felt confident about the academic side of the training—he was a very smart man. But he wasn't so sure about the physical portion, because it required him to stretch muscles he hadn't used in a while.

That's what he said—*lol!*

We both laughed about it. He'd joke and say, "I'm getting older, and I don't know how much of this stuff I can actually do!"

But then he got serious, and he did what he always did he put the Word on it. His favorite scripture:

"I can do all things through Christ which strengtheneth me." (Philippians 4:13, KJV)

When the time came for training, Gregory was ready and geared up. I believed in him wholeheartedly and did everything I could to support him throughout the process. And just as I knew God would bless him to do—he passed both parts with flying colors.

He was officially on his way to starting a new career—one that God had clearly ordained for him.

Chapter Eleven
Passion for His Career

As Gregory began his new career, he had little to no trouble forming strong relationships with his fellow coworkers. He loved everyone he encountered whether in the workplace, marketplace, community, or his neighborhood. He was no stranger to people, and it showed everywhere he went.

Whenever his rotating shift or team changed, Gregory adapted easily and never once complained. Not only did he get along with his coworkers, but he was also well-liked and respected by the inmates at the facility.

I remember how he would come home and share parts of his day with me laughing at some of the interactions he had. The inmates would often ask him to pray for them or to give them a "Word" from the Lord. Somehow, they found out he was a pastor just somehow… *ijs (I'm just saying)… lol.*

When they asked for prayer, Gregory would tell them he had prayed during his personal time with the Lord. A day or two later, they'd ask again, and he'd respond, "I already prayed for you!" To which they'd say, "Well, we need more prayer to get out of here."

And Gregory quick with a smile and a word would say, "No, you need more prayer to stay *out* of here!"

That always got a laugh. They also asked him for a "Word from the Lord." He would share what God placed on his heart, and they received it. But sure enough, a couple of days later, they'd come back: "Pastor Horne, you got another word for us?" And Gregory, being who he was, would say: "Why do you need another word? You haven't done anything with the last one I gave you!"

Again, the room would burst into laughter.

Though they were inmates, Gregory did his job professionally and respectfully. And in turn, they respected him. Many would "call on" Pastor Horne during their worst moments, and I would hear him at home faithfully praying for them.

While most of them respected him deeply, Gregory was wise enough to recognize that some did not. But even then, he knew how to watch and pray, managing those situations with the same grace and discernment. He continued to show God's love, regardless of how he was treated.

Gregory loved his career, and it suited him perfectly. He came to understand that his role was more than just a means of livelihood; it was part of his Kingdom assignment. It was part of his ministry.

He was faithful and dedicated, fully supporting the duties and functions of his department. He enjoyed attending:

- Christmas parties
- National Night Out events
- Back-to-school greeting events for children
- The SHINE Citizens Academy
- And other community-oriented programs

We even found ourselves attending some of those events together and we always enjoyed ourselves. Once again, Gregory's love for both family and commUNITY was evident.

One important thing I haven't yet mentioned is his deep Godly love, dedication, respect, and loyalty toward his Sheriff—Sheriff Cleveland "Clee" Atkinson.

Not a day or night went by that I didn't hear Gregory praying for the Sheriff, his coworkers, and yes even the inmates. It was a part of his daily routine. Gregory carried that burden in prayer faithfully, because he believed in covering them all before the Lord.

When I think about Gregory and his service, he truly exemplified his career with:

INTEGRITY, PROFESSIONALISM, and RESPECT.

He was:

- Dependable
- Kind
- Honest
- Trustworthy
- Compassionate
- Motivated
- Fair
- Accountable
- And always had a positive attitude

He honored the values of teamwork and leadership. He genuinely enjoyed his career and looked forward to going to work each day being surrounded by great coworkers, supportive staff, and even the very people (the inmates) he had come to respect and care for.

Chapter Twelve
Career Achievements and Promotion

Once again, Gregory loved everything about his career, and it showed through his hard work, dedication, and commitment. That same work ethic led to great honors, achievements, and a well-earned promotion.

In August 2017 and July 2020, Gregory was awarded "Detention Officer of the Month" along with several of his fellow coworkers. He was so excited and Godly proud of these achievements! When he came home, it was like watching a little kid showing off school awards. He was just that joyful.

To celebrate, I rewarded him with his favorite food, some good ole fried chicken.

What he didn't tell me at first was that, along with the award, he also received a gift card from Zaxby's. So yes, at some point, he got to enjoy extra chicken and he was so proud of himself!

Lord, have mercy... lol! So, between the award, the Zaxby's card, and his home celebration, he ended up receiving a triple reward and it brought him so much joy.

In June 2019, Gregory and several of his fellow officers received recognition for completing and passing the weeklong Armed Detention Officer Course. I knew without a doubt that he'd succeed—he was a studious and intelligent young man.

Gregory always gave his best. He applied himself fully to anything he took on and constantly strived for excellence. And when he needed a little extra motivation, he'd quote his favorite scripture:

> "I can do all things through Christ which strengtheneth me." (Philippians 4:13, KJV)

While working at the Sheriff's Office, Gregory decided to return to school. In 2017, he enrolled at Edgecombe Community College and earned Associate Degrees in:

- Criminal Justice Technology
- Human Services Technology

Throughout his college journey, he consistently made the Academic Honor Roll.

Gregory was determined to achieve those degrees, knowing they would support his professional growth at the Sheriff's Office. He never stopped trying to improve himself in every way possible. That's how much he loved his career.

Not long afterward, Gregory was promoted to Detention Corporal Officer.

Now, you talk about excitement—this man was so Godly proud and happy for what the Lord had blessed him to do! I always believed in him and knew he would receive that position in God's perfect timing.

And of course we celebrated! I made sure he knew how proud I was of him for every single achievement. I was his one and only best cheerleader, and I did everything I could to support and push him into each of his Kingdom purposes.

In his new position as Corporal, I witnessed even more growth and development in him. Gregory was incredibly teachable—he humbly allowed fellow coworkers to show him how to navigate the responsibilities of the role.

And not only was he teachable—he was a quick learner. He picked things up with ease and confidence.

As I watched him, I believed in my heart that elevation and promotion were coming for him again. I would tell him, and of course, his response was always:

"To God be all the glory."

When he said that, he was thanking God in advance—trusting that whatever God desired to do in his life would happen according to God's will and perfect timing.

Gregory continued to work in a spirit of excellence, remaining humble, honest, respectful, integral, loyal, dedicated, committed, and trustworthy.

He represented both God and his career with great honor.

Chapter Thirteen
That One Day That Shifted His Career

On August 16, 2022, it was Gregory's scheduled day off from work. However, a mandatory training had been scheduled, and so he attended.

Early in the training, during a break, Gregory called me and shared that everything was going well. As always, I encouraged him, and I prayed with him and for his fellow coworkers. He returned to continue his day.

Two hours later, he sent me a text and told me that, during his portion of the training, he had jumped over a four-foot fence and injured his right knee. My heart sank because he said it was very painful.

I asked if he had informed anyone about what had happened, and he said that he had. It was time for their lunch break, and so he came home.

When he arrived, I looked at his knee. It was slightly swollen, and he had pain when applying pressure to it. After lunch, he returned to the Training Center and was instructed to sit out the remainder of the physical training session.

Once training ended, he came back home this time in a lot of pain. I encouraged him to have it checked out, so we went to the local clinic, where he was examined and had x-rays performed.

Unfortunately, the results of the x-rays were not good.

Gregory was sent home with care instructions, pain medication, crutches, and a referral appointment with a local orthopedic specialist. He was instructed to stay out of work for two weeks until that appointment could be scheduled.

Gregory followed the instructions from the medical staff. However, two weeks passed before he was contacted about the referral appointment so he had to return to work on light duty.

A few days later, he finally received the call with his appointment details.

At that orthopedic appointment, he was examined and x-rayed again. The results were the same. The medical team gave him updated home care instructions and took him out of work again so that the fracture could heal properly and hopefully avoid surgery.

Gregory followed every instruction and was later scheduled for an MRI at a different medical facility in another town. The MRI confirmed the same results, and the medical team extended his out-of-work status once again.

At his next follow-up visit, they scheduled him to begin physical therapy.

Gregory was excited he was ready to get back to work.

As time went on and September arrived, Gregory continued following the doctors' instructions and patiently awaited his physical therapy. Other than the knee fracture, Gregory was a healthy person, and he was eager to regain his mobility.

We were both looking forward to the start of therapy. Gregory wasn't used to being immobile or unable to do the things he was used to doing—so this downtime was a real adjustment.

Yes, we were both hopeful and excited as we anticipated the start of physical therapy.

Chapter Fourteen
"The Leading Up" Days

I have always said that God is strategic in all that He does. And often, we do not understand it all at the moment. He is strategic because He knows the beginning and the end of all things—including our lives. He even knows all the middle parts.

He knows because He is God.

He is Omniscient, knowing and seeing all things.

He is Omnipresent, being everywhere at the same time.

He is Omnipotent, holding all power in His hands.

He is the True and Living God, and beside Him there is no other.

I say all of that to say this: the days leading up were strategic in so many ways. I didn't understand it back then but as time has passed, I can now better see and understand why God allowed things to unfold the way He did.

And for that, I bless Him.

Thank You, Lord!!!

While Gregory was out of work recovering, I found myself having to do many of the things he normally would, especially driving. I've never liked driving, particularly at night or for long distances. So one day I said to the Lord, "Lord, are you trying to teach me how to drive more?"

I shared that with Gregory, and we both just laughed.

I found myself doing a lot more than usual, but I didn't complain. I simply asked God to give me the strength to handle everything that needed to be done and He did just that.

I made sure Gregory followed the doctor's instructions closely so that he could heal properly from his injury.

Life continued to move forward, and God blessed us to keep going. We continued in ministry, and the Lord blessed His people in a mighty way.

There were a few ministry assignments I had scheduled before Gregory's injury, and though I wanted to cancel them to care for him, he encouraged me to keep them, assuring me he would be okay.

So I did.

Time passed, and one of those assignments was to minister at my classmate's church. The message was titled: "I Got Knocked Down, But I Didn't Stay Down." In it, I shared my personal journey through loss and grief.

This particular assignment had been scheduled around the same time our daughter, Alexus, was supposed to be coming home. I was so glad, knowing she would be there to support me with her presence and prayers.

She ended up coming home a few days earlier than planned, which was even better. Gregory and I were so happy to have her home, and we spent time catching up and enjoying each other's company.

I had also planned a cookout on that Saturday September 24th. I had prepped the food the night before, and now it was time to get the grill going. Alexus helped me with the grilling while Gregory rested.

We'd come inside and joke around with Gregory, laughing and enjoying one another. He was in good spirits and feeling well. It was truly an awesome weekend just being together and having fun.

When dinner was ready, we all sat down to eat. The food was delicious, and the laughter was abundant. It was one of those evenings where everything just felt *right*.

Later that night, Gregory mentioned that a relative had passed, and he really wanted to attend the viewing. Since he was still on crutches, Alexus drove him and helped him in and out of the vehicle.

I stayed behind to clean up and put all the food away.

When they returned home, everything was in order. The food was stored, the kitchen was clean, and the evening continued with more talking, laughing, and peaceful togetherness.

After a few hours, we all began to wind down and get ready for bed. I finished up my preparation for the assignment I was scheduled to minister the next day Sunday, September 25, 2022.

We were all happy, full, and settled in for the night. It had been a truly amazing day for us.

Chapter Fifteen
The Day and the Days That Changed My Entire Life

The Lord blessed us with a good night's rest. It was time for my daughter and me to get up and prepare for the assignment I had to fulfill. As I laid in bed, preparing to get up, I began to feel something in my spirit urging me to call the Pastor my classmate and let him know that I could not make it. I felt it strongly.

But eventually, I pushed myself up and proceeded to get ready.

It felt like a heaviness in my spirit, yet I pressed on.

While my daughter and I were getting ready, my husband got up and sat in the living room to see us off. That was nothing unusual; he always made sure to see us off whenever we left the house. He was such a caring and thoughtful gentleman toward us. That was just the kind of husband and father he was.

It was around 6:30 a.m. when we left the house. The assignment was scheduled for 8:00 a.m., but we left early because the Pastor wanted to meet with all the Ministers beforehand. The Lord blessed my daughter and me with safe travels, and we arrived on time. I met with the Pastor, his lovely wife, and the other Ministers as planned.

As always, I was excited and nervous, feelings I experience every time I have to minister.

After prayer, we all went out to begin the move of God.

As we sat together in preparation for the service, we had breakfast and shared introductions. It was a beautiful gathering of God's people, coming together in unity in the Lord's house.

Soon, the service began. The women of God began to minister, each sharing powerful personal testimonies. Then it was my turn.

My message was titled: "I Got Knocked Down, But I Didn't Stay Down."

The topic was incredibly fresh and personal to me, as the Lord had recently brought me through deep heartache and pain—losing several close family members, including my son, my mom, and my father-in-law.

The Lord blessed me to minister on the topic of death and grief. I shared:

- The physical aspect of how we handle death,

- The types and levels of grief, and how to manage them,

- And the spiritual perspective—what the Word of God says about how we are to go through these seasons.

(These points will be shared in more detail later in the book.)

I was able to share from my heart through personal testimony, Scripture, and even statistics. After every Minister had spoken, there was a time for the congregation to ask questions and share their own experiences. The fellowship was incredible.

Eventually, we came to the end. The Pastor and his wife expressed heartfelt gratitude to all the Ministers and those in attendance, and the service was dismissed.

Around 10:15 a.m., my daughter and I left the church and headed back home. On the way, I asked her to call into our ministry's conference call, because Apostolic Pastor Gregory was scheduled to deliver the Word at 10:00 a.m.

When she called in, no one was on the line which was unusual, as our calls typically lasted about an hour. But it had only been fifteen minutes.

We were concerned, but not overly worried at that moment. It didn't occur to us to call Gregory's phone. We just continued our drive home.

When we pulled into the driveway around 11:15 a.m., we sat in the truck for a moment, gathering our things. We were waiting for Gregory to come to the door, like he always did. That was his way of being loving, attentive, and thoughtful.

But this time, he didn't come to the door.

We weren't immediately alarmed. We thought maybe he had joined the conference call. So, we got out with our things and approached the door. I placed the key in the lock, turned it, and opened the door...

And there he was.

Gregory was lying on the floor in the hallway.

We both ran to him.

I began praying the Word of God over him, laying hands on him, and believing God for a miracle. I called 911, while my daughter stayed by his side doing all she knew to do.

As I was on the phone with the dispatcher, they guided me through CPR and checking for a pulse until help could arrive.

Even though I had CPR training as a caregiver, at that moment we were both overwhelmed, shocked, devastated, crying, and in utter disbelief. Our emotions were all over the place. We had just had a fun-filled weekend. He hadn't been feeling sick. Nothing seemed out of the ordinary.

Soon, paramedics, EMS, the fire department, and law enforcement arrived all around the same time. They immediately began working on Gregory.

My daughter and I began calling family members. The scene was heartbreaking.

One of Gregory's co-workers, Chief Deputy Gene Harrell, came to our home. He lived nearby and had heard about the emergency through his scanner. He was such a blessing. He stayed with us, helped calm us, and supported us in every way he could.

He even remained after family and friends arrived, helping me answer some of the questions from the First Responders. I was in no state of mind to respond clearly, and he stepped in for me. I will never forget that.

Then Gregory's cousin, more like a brother—Curmilus "Butch" Dancy II arrived. They had always been incredibly close. Butch, too, was in shock. I had never seen him cry until that day. He stayed by our side, comforting us however he could.

By now, the word had spread.

Neighbors, friends, church members, family, and even people we didn't know were calling, texting, and coming by. One of our neighbors just a few doors down came over and stayed with us. The street and yard were filled with people—all grieving, crying, and in disbelief.

I had to call my neighbors, Mr. and Mrs. Clifton Lashley, who weren't home at the time. Telling them was one of the hardest things I've ever done. But they returned immediately and stayed with us.

I couldn't bear the thought of calling our son, Lil Greg, so my daughter did. That was devastating for her and for him.

Everyone was in SHOCK, HURT, and PAIN. Many had just seen or spoken with him the day before. It didn't seem real then, and even two and a half years later it still doesn't feel real now. This heartbreaking and tragic event has been one of the worst moments of my entire life.

I've experienced loss before—my son, my mom, my father-in-law, and other relatives but this one shattered me to my core. That's not to say I didn't love my other family members deeply, but this loss was so sudden, so unexpected. Gregory wasn't sick. He was healthy, strong, vibrant—other than the knee injury from his work training.

Yes, this loss was devastating, traumatic, and deeply painful.

And as if that weren't enough, just two months later, on November 13, 2022, our adopted son Poncho passed away. Soon after that, my aunt (my dad's sister) passed. Then my father, and within two months of his passing, my uncle passed as well.

It has been a challenging and difficult season for me and my family. But through it all, the Lord continues to see us through day by day.

Corporal Gregory T. Horne

Sheriff Clee Atkinson, Jr. and the Edgecombe County Sheriff's Office sends our thoughts and prayers to the family and friends of Corporal Gregory T. Horne.

Chapter Sixteen
Lord, Why?

As I have done so many times even now, two and a half years later I still find myself asking the question:

"Lord, why?"

When I ask God this question, I don't do so in a negative way, nor am I questioning His sovereignty or why He chooses to do things the way He does. I simply ask for clarity and understanding, so that I can better accept His will and His plan concerning all that has happened.

Over the years, I've heard some people say that we are not to question God, but I'm so grateful that I now know better. We can ask God anything in His Son Jesus' name, and He will respond—according to John 16:23:

> *"And in that day ye shall ask Me nothing. Verily, verily, I say unto you, whatsoever ye shall ask the Father in My name, He will give it to you."*

All throughout the Bible, people asked God "why?"

- Job asked why he was suffering.

- David asked why God seemed distant.

- Even Jesus, on the cross, cried out, "My God, My God, why have You forsaken Me?"

- The prophet Habakkuk questioned God, saying: *"How long must I call for help?"* and *"Why do You make me look at injustice?"*

There are many more: Adam and Eve, Abraham, Sarah, Moses, Elijah, John the Baptist—and the list goes on.

So yes, it is okay to question God.

It doesn't mean we don't trust Him. It doesn't mean we are falsely accusing Him. Asking "why" is simply a human response when we seek understanding—when we desire to get to the root cause of a situation or pain that we don't yet understand.

And because God already knows our hearts, He also knows when we're going to question Him. And in His mercy and love, He prepares our hearts and minds to receive the answers—even if they come in parts, or over time.

I have asked God many "why" questions—and He has been so faithful to answer them. Not all at once, but graciously and consistently, in ways that have helped me find peace.

He loves us that much.

He answers us not only to give comfort, but to draw us closer to Him—so that we can rest in His purpose, even when it doesn't make sense to us at first.

God knows exactly what He is doing in each of our lives—and I bless Him for that.

As a matter of fact, the last sermon Apostolic Pastor Gregory ministered was titled:

"God Knows What He Is Doing!"

How *strategic* that message was. How *timely*, how *prophetic*—and now, how *foundational* it has become for me. That message is what I stand on every single day.

No matter what happens in life, I remind myself that: "God knows what He is doing," according to Jeremiah 29:11 (KJV):

"For I know the thoughts that I think toward you, saith the Lord, thoughts of peace, and not of evil, to give you an expected end."

So always remember this: You can ask God "why"—and He will answer you.

Not because He owes us anything, but because He loves us so deeply that He desires for us to walk in peace, trust, and faith in His perfect will.

Chapter Seventeen
Lord, Where Do I Go From Here?

I never thought in a million years that I would find myself being a widow.

When we got married, I just thought we would live and grow old together. I imagined us spending our lives loving our family, doing ministry, and enjoying life as husband and wife. Little did I know that my entire world would change in such a sudden and unexpected way.

My whole life shifted in a matter of five hours.

So, I had to cry out to the Lord. And the more I cried out, the more I felt His presence. He gave me peace and strength to start putting the pieces back together. My mind was racing with so many thoughts, but even in that overwhelming moment, God calmed and soothed me.

The Holy Spirit began to lead and guide me through the process—a process that was difficult physically, spiritually, and emotionally.

As I followed the leading of the Holy Spirit, I found myself leaning and depending on God Almighty like never before. I began to declare and decree the Word of

God over my life and situation. And just as Proverbs 3:5–6 says:

> *"Trust in the Lord with all thine heart; and lean not unto thine own understanding. In all thy ways acknowledge Him, and He shall direct thy paths."*

That Word became real to me.

The more I sought the Lord and followed His instructions, the more things started coming together. I followed the steps He gave me, and I found myself managing the responsibilities that needed my attention—not by my own strength, but through His grace.

I began to allow His Word to become my lifestyle. In fact, I found myself living His Word in real time.

The Holy Spirit gave me joy and laughter, even in the midst of sorrow, and that made the process easier to manage.

I had originally planned to draft this book much sooner, but the Lord gave me a different instruction.

He said,

"BE the book."

So I waited. And now, nearly two and a half years later, the Holy Spirit has released me to write it. He gave me the green light to author the book now—after living it.

Every day, I choose to let healing and wholeness be my portion.

Some days have been hard—and some still are—but God continues to carry me through.

At this point in my life, I'm seeing how the Lord is leading me forward. And it is truly because of His grace and mercy that I am still here and in my right mind.

Asking the Lord,

> "Where do I go from here?" has brought me into a place of greater peace, comfort, and strength.

I can see much clearer now. And God continues to prove Himself to me, again and again.

Chapter Eighteen
The Widow Life

My life as a widow has been a time of dealing with grief, navigating major life changes, adjusting to a lifestyle of solitude, and facing isolation from many—while still trying to rebuild my identity and rediscover my purpose.

Yes, it has been—and still is—a daily challenge. But I trust the process God has given me to follow.

Every day, I find ways to cope. That includes seeking support systems, though that too has been challenging at times. There were, and still are, days filled with sadness, loneliness, anger, depression, anxiety, and other overwhelming emotions—especially in the early stages following Gregory's transition.

Although I had already experienced the passing of my son, my mom, my father-in-law, and other dear relatives, this one hit differently. It wasn't because I loved them any less—but the loss of a spouse is an entirely different experience.

In those beginning days, my emotions were all over the place. But I knew I had to be strong for my children. It was the Holy Spirit who helped me manage my emotions.

He knew how to shift that sadness, anger, loneliness, and depression into a place of strength and power.

- That sadness became joy, and I received strength—for the joy of the Lord was, and still is, my strength.

- That anger transformed into peace and calm.

- The depression began to subside with the Word of God, the support of authentic friends and family, and professional counseling.

- The anxiety eased through my faith in God and other helpful coping tools.

- The loneliness was comforted by the abiding presence of the Lord. I held on to His promise: *"I will never leave nor forsake thee."*

- I had to learn how to manage the household finances alone. I had to adjust to living alone. I had to handle legal matters and make significant lifestyle changes—many of which I never imagined facing on my own.

I felt disconnected from some friends and family, simply because they couldn't understand the depth of a grieving spouse's pain. Some didn't know what to say, so they stayed away. There were people I had expected to see or hear from—but I didn't. Some, to this day, I've still not heard from. But you know what? I'm okay with that now.

Because in the end, God became and is my comforter and healer.

I've also come to understand that everyone has a role and a season in our lives. And while some may have stepped back, others stepped in with sincere prayers and unwavering support—for that, I am so grateful.

Even while grieving, I've had to make major life decisions. I've had to find new passions and interests to help fulfill my purpose.

To be fully transparent, being a widow has been—and continues to be—the hardest trial of my life. Gregory and I were married for almost eleven years—just two months shy of our anniversary. He wasn't just my husband. He was my best friend, ministry partner, prayer partner, lover, confidant, and soulmate.

He was a great provider and protector. He cooked, cleaned, did laundry, shopped, maintained the home and vehicles—you name it. When I was sick, he waited on me hand and foot. He loved God, his wife, his children, and his family. He loved everybody—even those who mistreated him. That was just who he was.

We were even the couple who dressed alike sometimes—especially for church services. We were tight y'all My healing journey has been challenging, especially with a limited social network. But God continues to place the right people at the right time in my life.

My children have been incredibly supportive—they call, text, and visit regularly, and I'm forever grateful. There are others, too, who've helped and continue to help. They bring meals, give rides, mow the lawn, or simply stop by for a visit. I thank God for every one of them.

Then there are those God placed in my life simply to bring fun and laughter. Two in particular—David and Sam— have meant more to me than they'll ever know. On some of my lowest days, these two had me laughing so hard that the Holy Spirit lifted my spirit.

Sadly, Sam recently passed away—just a few days after I wrote this portion of the book. His passing was deeply felt. But he lives on in my heart and in the hearts of many others.

R.I.P. Sam. You are loved and missed.

Death, Grief, and Mourning

Death is not the end. Some people believe that once we die, that's it. But Scripture teaches us differently.

While our earthly bodies return to dust, our souls will live forever—either in the presence of God or separated from Him. God doesn't want us to fear death or live in confusion or despair. Not everyone goes to the same place upon death.

According to Scripture, we will each go to one of two places:

- Those who have accepted Jesus will be in His presence for eternity.

- Those who have rejected Jesus and His grace will spend eternity in hell—a real place described in Scripture as one of darkness, fire, and separation.

When we lose someone, we are faced with overwhelming emotions and a new reality without them. But part of healing is to:

- Accept the reality of the loss

- Process the grief

- Adjust to life without them

- Remember them while still moving forward

These stages are necessary if we want to heal well and continue living with purpose.

I'm so thankful that during the loss of my closest loved ones, especially my husband, the Holy Spirit helped me walk through it.

Grieving doesn't mean we forget our loved ones. It means we hold them in our hearts while we heal—one day at a time.

Only God can do this kind of healing. And if we surrender to Him, He will carry us through.

For those of us who belong to Jesus, our goodbyes are never final. One day, we will see our loved ones again.

Hallelujah, Jesus!

I will see:

- My son, Demetrius

- My mom, Rosa Mae Everett Smith

- My mother- and father-in-law, Lula Rose and James Thomas Horne

- My brother-in-law, Wayne

- My beloved husband, Gregory

- My adopted son, "Poncho"

- My dad, Samuel Lee Lyons

- My Aunts: Sandy, Maxine, Peggy, Courtney, Edith, and Gertrude,

- My Uncles: Bernard, Jesse Jr., Bruce, Willard, and Robert Lee

- My Grandparents: Jesse and Rosa Lee Everett and Henry and Susie Lyons

Thank You, Lord!

My Healing Scriptures:

- Matthew 5:4 (KJV): *Blessed are they that mourn: for they shall be comforted.*

- Psalm 34:18 (KJV): *The Lord is nigh unto them that are of a broken heart; and saveth such as be of a contrite spirit.*

- Romans 12:15 (KJV): *Rejoice with them that do rejoice, and weep with them that weep.*

- 1 Peter 5:7 (KJV): *Casting all your care upon him; for he careth for you.*

- Philippians 4:7 (KJV): *And the peace of God, which passeth all understanding, shall keep your hearts and minds through Christ Jesus.*

- Ecclesiastes 3:4 (KJV): *A time to weep, and a time to laugh; a time to mourn, and a time to dance.*

- Psalm 30:5 (KJV): *Weeping may endure for a night, but joy cometh in the morning.*

- Psalm 34:1 (KJV): *I will bless the Lord at all times: his praise shall continually be in my mouth.*

Scripture references taken from THE HOLY BIBLE, KING JAMES VERSION, by Thomas Nelson.

While widowhood has brought comfort and grace, it's also brought some hard experiences. Some have taken advantage of my vulnerability—overcharging for services, breaking promises, or exploiting my kindness.

But I've learned to take those situations to the Lord. He shows me how to handle them with wisdom and grace.

Even in widowhood, God has been so good to me.

- When I'm weak, He makes me strong.

- When I'm lonely, He brings comfort.

- When I'm overwhelmed, He gives peace that surpasses all understanding.

- When I'm sad, He gives me laughter.

- When I'm confused, His Holy Spirit leads and guides me.

He is Jehovah Jireh—my Provider. He is my everything. And that's why I love Him so much.

Without God, I would never have made it this far. After all I've been through, He still keeps me in my right mind.

He is my All in All.

Chapter Nineteen
Not My Will But Thy Will Be Done

After all that God has allowed me to go through, I have made up my mind that His will shall be done in my life. I choose His will over my own desires.

I say this because God's way is always the better way, even when challenging times come into our lives.

Isaiah 55:8–9 (KJV) declares:

> *"For my thoughts are not your thoughts, neither are your ways my ways, saith the Lord.*
>
> *For as the heavens are higher than the earth, so are my ways higher than your ways, and my thoughts than your thoughts."*

I put God first in every aspect of my life because it is He who guides us on our daily paths on this journey called "life."

Matthew 6:33 (KJV) tells us:

"But seek ye first the kingdom of God, and his righteousness; and all these things shall be added unto you."

When I put God first in my life, "all things work together for good to them that love God, to them who are the called according to His purpose." (Romans 8:28, KJV)

I have learned that everything God allows us to go through in life has purpose, even when we don't fully understand it.

I didn't understand why He allowed my husband to leave in the way that he did. But as I've had time to seek the Lord, He has truly given me a better understanding of why He allowed it.

So yes—God's will be done, and not mine.

God knows exactly what He is doing in our lives, and I trust Him—even in the sudden and unexpected transitioning of my husband.

When I acknowledge that His plan and His ways are better, I can trust Him even more.

So, once again I say with confidence: Not my will, but Thy will be done!

Pain Produces Purpose

I have learned that pain produces purpose. I've learned that God knows everything that has happened and everything that will happen in our lives.

That's why He is:

- The Alpha and Omega

- The Way, the Truth, and the Life

According to:

- Revelation 22:13 (KJV): *"I am Alpha and Omega, the beginning and the end, the first and the last."*

- John 14:6 (KJV): *"Jesus saith unto him, I am the way, the truth, and the life: no man cometh unto the Father, but by me."*

Because God knows everything about us, we can trust Him with our lives.

I know that He is faithful and worthy of all my praise!

Even in my life as a widow—with all the challenges I've faced, and those that may come in the future—my testimony remains:

♪ There's a Story Behind My Praise

(Song by Carolyn Traylor, 2006)

> *There's a story behind my praise.*
> *That's why I'll continue to raise my hands.*
> *I'm gonna praise Him for the rest of my days.*
> *Oh, there's a story—yeah—behind my praise.*
> *There's a story behind my praise.*
> *That's why I'll continue to raise my hands.*
> *I'm gonna praise Him for the rest of my days.*
> *Oh, there's a story—yeah—behind my praise.*

_If you see me crying,
Oh, that is a story—
How He's been God to me in all of His glory.
Yeah, yeah, yeah, yeah...

If you see me shouting,
Oh, don't be amazed—
I just realized where and when I was saved.

If you see me running,
Oh, don't you think it strange—
My heart, He's rearranged.
There is a story behind my praise... my praise... my praise._

♪ I Feel Like Going On

(Song by Marvin Winans, 2010)

> *I feel like going on.*
> *Though trials may come on every hand,*
> *Oh, I feel like going on...*
>
> *Can I say it one more time?*
> *I feel like going on—*
> *(I don't know how you feel about it)*
> *I feel like going on... going on—*
> *Even though trials may come on every hand,*
> *I feel, I feel like going on.*
>
> *Come on, raise your hand if you've determined*
> *in your heart:*
> *"I'm going to go on, no matter what."*
> Sometimes you feel misguided,
> Sometimes you feel hurt,
> But you've got to keep going.
>
> *I feel like going on.*

Special Facebook Tributes

Linda Tharrington:

"Evangelist Teresa Everett Horne and Alexis Battle have my deepest sympathy in the loss of their husband and father, Gregory T. Horne. My condolences to their extended families, friends, and the Edgecombe County Sheriff's Department. Gregory Horne served Precinct 1-4 as Treasurer/Secretary for six years. We appreciate his service. Mr. Gregory T. Horne was such a good and gracious gentleman, a voice of sound reasoning. He will certainly be missed."

Purcell Jenkins (September 26, 2022):

"R.I.P. Words can't explain the amount of positivity and love you've shared with me throughout high school and college. If not the first, for sure the second to comment and message me about my music and education—just to make sure I was doing good and to encourage me to keep going 100. And for that, I thank you. Until we meet again, Big Cuzzo. #drumline #GregoryTHorne"

James Clay (September 26, 2022):

"Praying for the family. He was always respected and will be missed."

Cody Medford (September 26, 2022):

"Fixed a car for him about two months ago… super nice guy. Praying for Evangelist Teresa Everett Horne and family."

TJ Marks (September 26, 2022):

"I stayed across the street from him for 10 years. The kindest man I've had the pleasure of meeting. This hurt me today seeing this. My prayers go out to his family."

Shawn Lake (September 26, 2022):

> "I'm a pretty private person. I don't post a lot on social media and I tend to keep my emotions to myself—but this one hurt. I found out today at work that Mr. Horne passed away over the weekend. At first, I wanted to believe it had to be a mistake… that it couldn't be true. But unfortunately, it was, and my heart has been heavy ever since getting the news.
>
> I can count on one hand the number of people in this world that I have as much respect for as I do for him.

If you've never worked in a detention center, it's not an easy job. You're called every name in the book. Some inmates will threaten you and your family, try to get under your skin, and yes, sometimes unfortunately, things get physical. Gregory T. Horne always treated people fairly. He faced all of these situations with the kind of grace that let you know he wasn't just a 'religious person' like so many others—he lived what he preached. He cared about his community and people in general, and you could see that what he had was real.

I'm a pretty thick-skinned guy, but I remember just like it was yesterday—working with Mr. Horne when an inmate was doing his absolute best to make me lose it. He mentioned my kids, and I was one breath away from crossing a line. Mr. Horne looked at me and said: "Don't give him what he wants. You're too smart for that. You're better than that."

The following week, that same man turned his attention to Mr. Horne and said practically everything a man could say to get him angry. I could see the anger in Mr. Horne's face, but he responded by telling the man he would pray for him. As I walked by, I repeated to Mr. Horne the same wise words he had told me the week before. He smiled.

One of the worst things about growing older is that I won't get to run into Mr. Horne in Food Lion anymore when I happen to be shopping with the kids. I'm going to miss that. Hearing that he was gone felt like a punch in the gut. I can't even imagine how it feels for his wife and family.

If by chance any of you see this, please know that he was highly respected and admired by a lot of people. I considered working with him an honor. Regardless of how anyone feels about religion or law enforcement, this community—and all of Edgecombe County—was a safer and better place with Mr. Horne here.

If all of us were half the man that he was, this world would be a better place. Please keep his family in your thoughts and prayers. I'm going to miss you...."

Children's Tribute

Alexus Battle (March 5, 2025):

"I remember the very first day I met Greg! It seems like it was just yesterday. He had brought my Mom a new refrigerator for her house. When he finally left, I asked my Mom, 'Who was that man?' (LOL) She told me that was her friend, and I said okay! But I knew it was more than just a 'friend!'

I also remember the first time Greg asked me if I wanted something to eat before he came over to my Mom's house. I was like, 'Oh yes! I sure do. You don't have to ask me twice, my boy.' I wanted a 3-piece chicken strip meal from McDonald's with a Sprite and honey mustard sauce. Once he came over and gave me the food, I was lit — like a kid in a candy store! Greg became cool in my book after that. LOL!

Next thing I knew, my Mom told me she was getting married. I really didn't know how to accept that. Of course, I was happy for her. She deserved all the love, happiness, and joy in the world! But it was hard for me to process — not because she was getting married, but because:

1. Someone else would now be in our household.

2. I would have a father figure — not only in the home but in my life.

Can you imagine going almost 12 or 13 years of your life living in a single-parent household, only having a consistent relationship with your Mom, to now having a two-parent household? Exactly. So, it was a really hard conversation to process in the moment.

There's one conversation in particular I will NEVER forget having with Greg. He came and sat down with me one day and said, *'I'm not trying to replace your father, but I am here to be a father to you.'*

Y'all... when I say I was speechless... Just hearing those words gave me so much comfort. What I had been longing for — for so long — was now happening. I was finally getting that father-daughter relationship I'd always desired.

I could go on and on about everything — it would take all day. Greg was one of the best people I could have ever come across in my life. He was such a humble, God-fearing, kindhearted person you could ever encounter. He was soft-spoken, a gentle type of man, but he would "get right" if he had to — which was hardly ever (LOL).

He loved God, his wife, his kids, and his family. Greg was truly a family man! After God, his family was his top priority. I know no one on earth is perfect, but Greg was close to it. You just had to know him to understand that.

There are so many memories I shared with Greg. I remember when I first got my license — Greg would always want me to back my car in versus pulling in. I hated backing in because it took too much effort, and most importantly, I really didn't know how to do it (LOL). But after a few practices, I had it down pat. So now, all I do is back in. Shout out to Greg for staying on me about that and not letting me give up. (In case y'all didn't know — people who back their vehicles in are really cool! LOL!)

Greg had me SPOILED ROTTEN! When my Mama would say "no" or give me an answer I didn't like, I would go right to Greg — and he would always say, "Yes, Homie," or give me an answer I did like. He never told me "no" (LOL).

Greg showed up for everything that involved me — from school-related things to moments in my adult life.

- He was there when I got my first car.

- He was there when I received my college acceptance letters.

- He was there during all my graduations.

- He was there when I moved into my first place.

He was always there. He never missed a beat. He was just what I needed in my life. He was truly an amazing father.

Life changed a little when I moved two hours away from home. Although I wasn't in my parents' household anymore, the love and communication never stopped. I literally talked to my Mom and Greg every day — multiple times a day. You would have thought I was the parent and they were my kids (LOL). I just needed to make sure they were good. I would put that Kia on two wheels down that highway if I needed to! Haha!

But seriously though — the only thing that separated us was the distance. I missed my parents, but it was the appointed time for me to step out and soar! I would occasionally come back home for special occasions and holidays. I made sure I came back to the 252!

Time passed, and then came the weekend of September 23, 2022. I will never forget it. I lost one of the closest people to me. I lost a piece of my heart. The images are still in my mind. I don't think I'll ever be able to erase those moments — no matter how hard I try.

As I've navigated these years, I've come to realize I need Greg now in my young adulthood more than I did in my teens. There have been so many times where I wish I could call him — even with him being two hours away — and tell him what I needed. Although it wouldn't always make sense for him to drive two hours, I knew he would've come. Remember, he never told me "no" (LOL).

There are so many things I need his advice on... his guidance. There is nothing like a father's love. The years I shared with him just weren't enough. I'm thankful for them, but I needed more time.

I write this tribute to express my love, gratitude, and heartfelt feelings that I had toward Greg. I pray that one day the man I marry will be just like Greg — or even better.

Greg, you will forever be in my heart. I love and miss you so much.

Love,

Your daughter,
Alexus aka Homie

Gregory Thomas Horne Jr. (March 15, 2025):

"To the man who made me a man.

Not a day goes by that I'm not grateful for every lesson you gave me.

Not a day goes by that I don't think about you.

I love and miss you so much, and you'll always be on my mind and in my heart.

Love,

Your son,
Greg Jr.

My Special Family Tribute

I take this opportunity to pay special tribute to our immediate family members who have transitioned. I deeply miss them all, and I know that God has not — and will not — put more on me than I can bear. He is such a faithful God, who is my refuge and strength, a very present help in trouble, according to:

> Psalm 46:1 (KJV): *"God is our refuge and strength, a very present help in trouble."*

It is His joy that gives me strength from day to day. It is His peace that surpasses all understanding that guards my heart and mind daily, according to:

> Philippians 4:7 (KJV): *"And the peace of God, which passeth all understanding, shall keep your hearts and minds through Christ Jesus."*

It is in Him that I live, and move, and have my being, as declared in:

> Acts 17:28 (KJV): *"For in him we live, and move, and have our being..."*

And I find great comfort in this blessed assurance of reunion:

1 Thessalonians 4:16–17 (KJV):

"For the Lord himself shall descend from heaven with a shout, with the voice of the archangel, and with the trump of God: and the dead in Christ shall rise first:

Then we which are alive and remain shall be caught up together with them in the clouds, to meet the Lord in the air: and so shall we ever be with the Lord."

In Loving Memory

- Demetrius Devon Everett (Son) – *November 22, 2017*

- Rosa Everett Smith (Mother) – *April 30, 2020*

- James Thomas Horne (Father-in-Law) – *December 13, 2020*

- Lula Rose Hussey Horne (Mother-in-Law) – *October 24, 2003*

- Dennis Wayne Hussey (Brother-in-Law) – *December 27, 1991*

- Gregory Thomas Horne Sr. (Husband) – *September 25, 2022*

- Francisco "Poncho" Guerrero (Adopted Son) – *November 13, 2022*

- Samuel Lee Lyons (Father) – *October 1, 2024*

My Special Family Tribute goes out to ALL of my family who have gone on years before the publishing of this book. No one shall be forgotten. They ALL rest upon my heart daily.

Rest in Peace

You are forever in our hearts and never forgotten.

The Life of Gregory Thomas Horne Sr.

About the Author

Prophet Evangelist Pastor Teresa Everett Horne, a native of Tarboro, North Carolina, is the widow of Apostolic Pastor and Detention Corporal Officer Gregory Thomas Horne Sr. She is the proud mother of two adult children, Alexus and Greg Jr.

She is an Ordained Prophet, Evangelist, and Pastor in the Lord Jesus Christ, walking under a powerful prophetic and apostolic anointing in both her evangelistic and pastoral callings. She boldly preaches the Gospel of the Kingdom of God and is committed to fulfilling the Great Commission. She is the Pastor of EndTime Harvest Outreach Ministries and the Founder/ Trailblazer of Kingdom Impact Resource Center Inc. in Tarboro, North Carolina.

Prophet Evangelist Pastor Teresa Everett Horne is a God-fearing woman who passionately loves the Lord and His people. She carries a soul-winning anointing upon her life. She is an anointed servant, encourager, intercessor, visionary, author, and prayer warrior. Despite enduring profound personal loss and seasons of suffering, she continues to stand firmly on the promises of Almighty God, daily proclaiming:

"To God Be All the Glory!"

Made in the USA
Columbia, SC
19 January 2026

77520509R00065